MEGAFAST

Buckle up and explore some of the fastest machines ever made!

First published in 2024 by Hungry Tomato Ltd
F15, Old Bakery Studios, Blewetts Wharf, Malpas Road,
Truro, Cornwall, TR1 1QH, UK

Thanks to our creative team
Senior Graphic Designer: Amy Harvey
Editor: Holly Thornton
Editor: Millie Burdett

Beetle Books is an imprint of Hungry Tomato.

ISBN 9781916598591

Printed and bound in China
Discover more at:
www.mybeetlebooks.com
www.hungrytomato.com

Picture Credits
(abbreviations: t = top; b = bottom; m = middle; l = left; r = right; bg = background)

Shutterstock: 360b 78br; Artur Didyk 9br; Asharkyu 74 tr; Austin Deppe 76 tr; Bruce Alan Bennett 77tr; Corina Huter 78tl; Darunrat Wongsuvan 6mr; DigitalPen 9bl; Evannovostro 74br; EvrenKalinBacak 79bl; Franck Boston 76ml, 79bm; Grindstone Media Group 74ml; Ilya_Levchenko 7tl; Kletr 76br; Kristen Greenwood 78bm; Lassedesignen 6tl; Logan Bush 79tl; Luckyluke007 77br; Marek Pelikan 75br; MaRRitch 78bl; Open Studio 1bg, 8tl; ParabolStudio 8mr; Sue Thatcher 75ml; Supamotionstock.com 7bl; Vs148 7mr, 75tr; YIUCHEUNG 2-3bg, 9tl. NASA/DFRC (Wikipedia) 77ml.

Every effort has been made to trace the copyright holders and we apologize in advance for any unintentional omissions. We would be pleased to insert the appropriate credit in any subsequent edition of this publication.

MEGAFAST

Written by John Farndon

Illustrated by Mat Edwards and Jeremy Pyke

CONTENTS

TERRIFIC CARS

AMAZING PLANES

MIGHTY MONSTER TRUCKS

Words in **BOLD** can be found in the glossary.

WHAT IS MEGAFAST?

Buckle up for a wild ride as we explore some of the fastest machines in the world!

MEASURING SPEED

It's easy to see when a vehicle is megafast, but how do you know just how fast it is? The most accurate way of measuring top speed is to measure how long a vehicle takes to cover an exact distance, like a mile (or km!).

TESTING THE LIMITS

In most countries, main roads have speed limits of around 70 mph (113 km/h) - that's fast enough for most people! But all the bikes in this book can go way faster than that. That means they only reach their top speeds on private roads and racetracks, where they can push themselves to the limits.

LOOKING THE PART

Speed machines aren't just megafast - they also look super cool! Like the Dodge Tomahawk, many bikes are modified to look unique and memorable, as well as to be really quick.

ENGINE POWER

To achieve impressive top speed stats and compete among the world's fastest, the cars in this book all have super powerful engines. They're measured in **torque**, which shows how hard a vehicle can **accelerate**, and **horsepower (hp)**, which shows how quickly the vehicle moves during acceleration.

BREAKING RECORDS

High torque and hp mean faster movement, higher top speeds, and a better chance of winning races, breaking world records and becoming the king or queen of speed! Drivers around the world are always trying to break records and become famous. That means records and stats are constantly changing!

SUPER SPEEDY SAFETY

With super speed comes lots of danger! The record holders and speedsters you'll read about in this book have had years of driving training. They also have to wear safety gear like multiple seat belts, helmets and gloves to protect them in case they crash, especially in big competitions like Top Fuel and NASCAR.

FAST FLYERS

If you truly want to go megafast, you must fly. Up in the air, there's very little to get in your way! Many of the aerial speedsters in this book can zoom through the sky at incredible speeds.

SPEEDY SOARERS

Speed is usually measured in mph or km/h. But many rockets and planes can soar over several km per second! For the speediest machines, it makes more sense to compare them to the speed of sound. A plane flying at the speed of sound (typically over 700 mph/1,127 km/h) is said to be flying at **Mach** 1. It's very rare for land vehicles to go this fast!

PREPARE FOR LAUNCH

Some planes are able to take off by speeding along a runway and launching themselves into the sky. Others – mostly the super speedy rocket-powered aircraft in this book – are dropped in the sky by bigger rockets! This is a clever way to conserve fuel.

AWESOME ACCELERATION

Another way of seeing how fast something moves is to measure how quickly it gains speed – that's acceleration. For megafast vehicles, this is measured by how long it takes to reach a certain speed from a standing start.

There are some impressive 0-60 mph (0-97 km/h) stats in this book!

TERRIFIC TRUCKS

Once, being megafast belonged just to bikes, cars and planes, but now trucks have joined the fun – giant rigs, pickups, monster stunt wagons, fire trucks… you name a truck and certainly someone somewhere is racing it at top speed! And, they normally look pretty cool while they do it.

Fasten your seat belt and prepare to have your breath taken away…!

HONDA'S SUPER BLACKBIRD

For 6 years, Kawasaki's Ninja ZX-11 held the title of world's fastest production bike. Honda was annoyed by this; it was determined to make an even faster bike! It claimed the title with its CBR1100XX Super Blackbird. For 2 years, it held the title with a mighty speed of 178 mph (286 km/h) - until Suzuki fought back with the Hayabusa, which was faster still...

INLINE

Motorcycle engines are identified by the layout and number of cylinders – the tubes in which fuel burns to produce power. The layouts are usually either in a V-shape or in a line, with two or four cylinders. The Honda Blackbird is an inline-four.

JUST LIKE A JET PLANE

The Blackbird was named after the Lockheed SR-71 Blackbird **reconnaissance** jet of the 1970s (see page 48). The SR-71 was a record-breaker, too: it's one of the world's fastest and highest-flying jet planes! It could rocket through the air at 2,193 mph (3,529 km/h) and, in 1974, it roared from New York to London in less than two hours. Wow!

POWER
168 hp

0-60 MPH (0-97 KM/H)
2.8 seconds

TOP SPEED
178 mph
(286 km/h)

ENGINE
1137 **cc**
inline-four

TORQUE
92 lb-ft
(124 **Nm**)

SUPERFAST SUZUKI

When Suzuki designed the streamlined shape for the Hayabusa, it was inspired by a swooping bird of prey. The bike it built is a predator of the road. Hayabusas made in 1999 could reach up to 194 mph (312 km/h), breaking speed records for production models and starting a "speed war" between bike manufacturers!

THE FASTEST BIRD

Hayabusa is the Japanese word for peregrine falcon. The peregrine dives toward its prey at incredible speeds of 200 mph (322 km/h), making it the fastest of all animals. The peregrine also preys on blackbirds – when it was launched in 1999, the Suzuki Hayabusa overtook Honda's "Super Blackbird" as the world's fastest production bike.

POWER
175 hp

**0-60 MPH
(0-97 KM/H)**
2.5 seconds

TOP SPEED
194 mph
(312 km/h)

ENGINE
1299 cc
inline-four

TORQUE
98 lb-ft
(133 Nm)

TAME BEAST

Many riders and superbike fans think the Hayabusa is the best superbike ever. It's not just that it's fantastically fast. The bike also handles speeds with ease, and it runs remarkably smoothly for such a powerful bike. It's just as at home on city streets as wild mountain roads. It's no surprise that the second- and third-generation Hayabusas are just as popular as the first.

JET-POWERED STORMER

Prepare for takeoff! The MTT Y2K looks like an ordinary motorcycle, but it's powered by a Rolls-Royce M250 jet turbine that's usually used in helicopters. There have been a few special jet-powered bikes propelled by the jet's thrust of hot air alone. But the Y2K's turbine is different: it's built to run on the roads just like any other bike. It's an ordinary bike with extraordinary power!

HOW DOES IT WORK?

In the Y2K's turboshaft engine, air is swept into the front and squeezed by a fan, mixed with fuel and set alight by a spark. The burning mix swells rapidly and blasts backward to turn another fan, turning the shaft that drives the back wheel.

WHAT DOES Y2K MEAN?

Y2K is the millennium or Year 2 Thousand (K is short for *kilo*, which is Greek for "thousand"), the year that the MTT Y2K was launched.

TWO-WHEEL BLAST

When the Y2K was launched in 2000, its performance was terrifying. It could reach 200 mph (322 km/h) in just 5.4 seconds. This technology had never been seen before, and the bike set records for its strength and power. An even more powerful version, the MTT 420RR launched in 2015, is claimed to hit over 275 mph (443 km/h)! See its amazing stats in the right-hand bar.

POWER
420 hp

0-60 MPH (0-97 KM/H)
2.5 seconds

TOP SPEED
275 mph
(443 km/h)

ENGINE
197 cc
gas turbine

TORQUE
500 lb-ft
(678 Nm)

FLYING TOMAHAWK

The Dodge Tomahawk must be one of the most stand-out superbikes ever. Dodge claimed its megapowerful engine would slam it over 300 mph (483 km/h). If this were true, it would be the fastest superbike in the world! But no one has ever dared to try it beyond 100 mph (161 km/h).

MOTORCYCLE OR CAR?

What makes the Tomahawk so powerful is its huge car engine. To carry this weight, the bike hasn't got two wheels but four! Experts have debated whether this makes it more of a car. But they now agree that its styling – one seat, handlebars and handbrakes – makes it a bike.

DON'T MOVE!

The Tomahawk was launched in 2003, but only nine have ever been built. And none can be legally ridden on the road. Dodge say its bike is a "**rolling sculpture**" and not meant to be ridden seriously. At high speeds, a rider will be blown off, as it has no **protective fairing**!

POWER
500 hp

0-60 MPH (0-97 KM/H)
2.5 seconds

TOP SPEED
420 mph
(676 km/h)
in your dreams!

ENGINE
8.3L
V10 twin-
turbocharged

TORQUE
525 lb-ft
(712 Nm)

FLYING BLADE

The Tomahawak gets its name from a kind of axe first used long ago by the native peoples of North America. The original native tomahawks were stone, but when the Europeans arrived, the stone was replaced by a metal blade. Warriors could throw these axes with deadly speed and accuracy.

SHIMMERING LOTUS

When racing car specialist Lotus began building superbikes, it came up with the C-01. With a 200 hp V-twin engine, it's superpowerful, and Lotus calls it a hyperbike. But it's the supersleek carbon **"monocoque"** body shell that really catches the eye. It was created by German designer Daniel Simon, who designed the "light cycles" in the science fiction movie *Tron*.

FORMULA ONE STYLE
Lotus is also a famous name in **Formula One (F1)** racing. In the 1960s, famous drivers such as Jim Clark and Graham Hill won race after race in Lotus cars. The design for the C-01 bike was inspired by the Lotus 49 F1 racing car driven by Hill and Clark.

LOTUS FLOWER

The Lotus company was created by racing driver Colin Chapman in 1952. No one knows why he chose the name Lotus. The lotus plant is sacred in many parts of tropical Asia, where it grows in ponds. Its flower is also a symbol of elegance, beauty and grace.

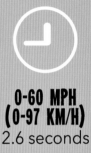

POWER
200 hp

0-60 MPH (0-97 KM/H)
2.6 seconds

TOP SPEED
200 mph
(322 km/h)

ENGINE
1195 cc
V-twin

TORQUE
Unknown

KAWASAKI NINJA

Kawasaki's Ninja H2 is one of the fastest street-legal bikes ever, with a potential top speed of 209 mph (336 km/h) and a punchy 200 hp. A special supercharged engine forces a mighty 310 hp out of the race version, the H2R. In 2016, the bike's speed record was broken when rider Kenan Sofuoglu hit 248 mph (399 km/h)!

BURN UP

To handle the H2's power, Kawasaki put a lot of technology into the bike's brakes, suspension and launch control. The electronic traction control system adjusts the power delivery to the wheel if it starts to slip when the rider is accelerating out of a bend.

LEGENDARY NAME

Kawasaki uses the name Ninja for its fastest bikes. Ninjas were spies and assassins in Japanese history. They dressed in dark blue to keep hidden at night and were famous for their speed, stealth and ability to kill silently. Their skill in climbing and getting into impossible places was legendary.

POWER
310 hp

**0-60 MPH
(0-97 KM/H)**
2.9 seconds

TOP SPEED
248 mph
(399 km/h)

ENGINE
998 cc
supercharged
inline-four

TORQUE
122 lb-ft
(165 Nm)

ON THE FAST TRACK

If you want to go fast on a bike, the best place is on a racetrack. MotoGP, short for Motorcycle Grand Prix, has the fastest races of all. In MotoGP, riders hurtle around flat tracks on purpose-built bikes at speeds of up to 225 mph (362 km/h). They corner at high speeds by leaning far off their bikes to keep them balanced – so far that one knee will scrape the ground!

GOING FOR THE RECORD

MotoGP bikes must conform to strict rules to make sure that riders compete fairly. The maximum permitted engine size is 1000 cc, for example, and the maximum number of cylinders is four. MotoGP bikes are driven so hard and fast that their engines often need replacing! Riders are limited to 7 engines per season.

MOTOGP CIRCUITS

In the 2022 season, 21 MotoGP races took place across 17 different countries including Indonesia, where riders got to race on the new Mandalika International Street Circuit. With new speed records set, the bikes really are getting faster every year!

POWER
240 hp

0-60 MPH (0-97 KM/H)
2.6 seconds

TOP SPEED
225 mph
(362 km/h)

ENGINE
Limited to 1000 cc inline-four

TORQUE
Over 88 lb-ft
(over 120 Nm)

STRIPPED FOR SPEED

When racing car designer Gordon Murray built the McLaren F1 in 1991, he wanted it to be the fastest road car ever. He stripped the car down to essentials to keep it light, and added a super powerful engine. To stop the mega-engine from overheating, the bay is lined with pure gold - the best heat deflector there is!

The bird on McLaren's badge is a kiwi bird, a symbol of New Zealand, birthplace of company founder Bruce McLaren.

MIDDLE OF THE ROAD?

Most supercars have just two seats. But the F1 has three. The driver sits in front in the middle, with the passengers either side and slightly behind. This position gives the driver unusually good visibility.

POWER
627 hp

**0-60 MPH
(0-97 KM/H)**
3.2 seconds

TOP SPEED
240 mph
(386 km/h)

ENGINE
6.1L V12
(BMW)

TORQUE
480 lb-ft
(650 Nm)

BUILT FOR SPEED

The F1 outgunned all other cars of the time with a top speed of 240 mph (386 km/h), a record not beaten for nearly a decade. Faster cars have been built since with supercharged, turbo engines, but the F1 remains the fastest **naturally aspirated** car on the planet!

BUGATTI'S GRAND MASTER

The Bugatti Veyron is fast - very, very fast! In fact, it held the title of "fastest production car in the world" for 7 years! It may have been beaten by the Agera (page 28), but it's still legendary. It's about 5 times as powerful as an average family car. With that kind of muscle, it can reach nearly 270 mph (435 km/h)! That's so fast it needs special aerodynamic shaping to stop it from taking off!

Bugatti Veyron

BURN-UP

At top speed, the Veyron's tires/tyres only last 15 minutes! Its fuel tank goes dry in 12 minutes. Its engine also consumes as much air as one person breathes in four days.

THE FIRST SUPERCAR?

In 1936, Bugatti made the super sleek 57SC Atlantic. SC stood for "**supercharger**", which increases the supply of compressed air to an engine. This meant the 57SC could reach 120 mph (193 km/h), which was incredibly fast compared with other cars of the 1930s. For this reason, many people call it the world's first supercar. Its speed isn't as impressive today, but its beautiful streamlined body is.

57SC Atlantic

POWER
987 hp

0-60 MPH (0-97 KM/H)
2.5 seconds

TOP SPEED
269 mph (433 km/h)

ENGINE
8L W16 cylinders, turbocharged

TORQUE
922 lb-ft (1,250 Nm)

VIKING THUNDER

A thousand years ago, the Viking people of Sweden were awed by Thor, god of Thunder. Now awesome thunder bursts out of Sweden in the roar of the Koenigsegg Agera R, one of the world's fastest production cars. Agera means "take action" - and the Agera can accelerate from 0 to 60 mph (0-97 km/h) in just 2.8 seconds to reach an incredible 278 mph (447 km/h).

STOP!

With such fast cars, good brakes are vital, and the Agera's are phenomenal. It holds the world record for blasting from a standstill to an impressive 249 mph (401 km/h), then screeching to a halt again - all in just 28.1 seconds.

NEWSFLASH

Koenigsegg has started producing cars which can use both fuel and electric power. Its newer car, the Regera, uses both seamlessly, making it a super fast, smooth ride that's much more eco-friendly.

POWER
1,100 hp

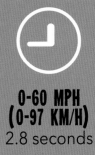

0-60 MPH (0-97 KM/H)
2.8 seconds

TOP SPEED
278 mph
(447 km/h)

ENGINE
5L V8 twin-turbocharged

TORQUE
885 lb-ft
(1,200 Nm)

GHOST RIDER

The Agera's interior has eerie "ghost light" controls. LED lights seem to appear out of nowhere on solid metal buttons. The light shines through almost invisible micro-holes.

FIGHTING FAST

Sharply creased and flat, the Lamborghini Aventador is unusually shaped for a car, but it fits right in next to the incredible aircraft it was inspired by - the Lockheed F-117 Nighthawk. The F-117 was the world's first stealth fighter plane. Its unusual flat surfaces made it almost invisible to radar waves; it could fly undetected by enemies! With impressive acceleration, the Aventador also vanishes quickly...

LAMBO DOORS

One of the special features of the Aventador is its Lamborghini trademark "scissor doors", sometimes known as "Lambo doors". Unlike gullwing doors that swing out and up, scissor doors pivot straight upward at the front, to open like a scissor blade.

NEW AND NEWER

Lamborghini has carried on making newer models of the Aventador, each better than the one before. The most recent model, released in 2021, is the fastest yet, topping 220 mph (354 km/h)! Check out its amazing stats to the right.

POWER
770 hp

**0-60 MPH
(0-97 KM/H)**
2.9 seconds

TOP SPEED
220 mph
(354 km/h)

ENGINE
6.5L V12

TORQUE
531 lb-ft
(720 Nm)

FAST AS A SNAKE

The Hennessey Venom GT was always megafast. But its follow-up, the F5 Venom, is even faster! Twin **turbochargers** give the V8 engine a scary 1,800 hp of power, and the car body is strong but incredibly lightweight. The F5 absolutely blows the Koenigsegg Agera R away, with a top speed over 310 mph (499 km/h)!

THE FURY OF A TORNADO

The F5 was named after the most powerful tornado of all on the **Fujita scale**. Winds rip round an F5 tornado at over 200 mph (322 km/h). So the F5 Venom and a tornado are a perfect match!

VEYRON V VENOM

On one particular whirlwind run in 2014, the Venom GT roared up to 270.5 mph (435 km/h). That made it faster than the record-breaking Veyron's 269 mph (433 km/h). But the Venom only made the run one way, not two ways. This meant that the Veyron held on to its crown as the world's fastest production car… just!

POWER
1,800 hp

**0-60 MPH
(0-97 KM/H)**
2.7 seconds

TOP SPEED
Over
310 mph
(499 km/h)!

ENGINE
7L V8
twin-turbo

TORQUE
1,155 lb-ft
(1,566 Nm)

JET-PROPELLED

If you want to break the world land speed record, you need jet power. That's what the world's fastest cars - the successful record breakers - used. The record holder is still Richard Noble's Thrust SSC, which reached 763 mph (1,228 km/h) in October 1997, driven by Andy Green. It was so fast it broke the sound barrier, moving faster than sound!

North American Eagle

Bloodhound SSC

SPIRIT OF AMERICA

American Craig Breedlove loved speed. After a successful career as a racing driver, he turned to the land speed record – and broke it five times in cars called Spirit of America. In 1964, Breedlove became the first person to drive at over 500 mph (805 km/h). In 1965, he became the first to reach 600 mph (966 km/h), and his wife Lee Breedlove drove at 308 mph (496 km/h), making them the fastest couple on Earth…

POWER
110,000 hp

**0-60 MPH
(0-97 KM/H)**
2.8 seconds

TOP SPEED
763 mph
(1,228 km/h)

ENGINE
Two
Rolls-Royce
turbofans

THRUST
50,000 lb-ft
(67,800 Nm)

GOING FOR THE RECORD

Thrust SSC (above) still holds the world land speed record. It went from 0 to 600 mph (0-966 km/h) in just 16 seconds! But many other cars have tried to beat it, including the North American Eagle, Aussie Invader and Bloodhound SSC. They hope to reach 1,000 mph (1,609 km/h) but haven't managed it yet!

THE WHEEL THING

Up until 1963, all land speed records were achieved in cars driven by their wheels, like ordinary road cars. Then Craig Breedlove broke the record in a jet-propelled car. Since then, all record-breakers have been jet-propelled. But there are still people who want to make wheel-driven cars travel at mega-high speeds.

Bluebird CN7

RECORD-BREAKERS

In this line-up are three amazing record-breakers. On the left is Donald Campbell's Bluebird CN7, the last wheel-driven car to hold the land speed record, of 403.1 mph (649 km/h) in 1964. In the middle is Buckeye Bullet, a battery-powered car built by Ohio students that reached 307.7 mph (495 km/h). Coming up fast in the background is George Poteet's Speed Demon.

Speed Demon

Buckeye Bullet

POWER
3,155 hp

**0-60 MPH
(0-97 KM/H)**
Unknown

TOP SPEED
482 mph
(776 km/h)

ENGINE
V8 twin-turbo

WHIZZING WHEELS

In 2012, American George Poteet fired the Speed Demon up well over 400 mph (644 km/h) across Bonneville Salt Flats, setting a world record for a piston-engined, wheel-driven car. Every year, the team makes the car faster. In 2020, it topped its past world record by exceeding 480 mph (772 km/h)! See Speed Demon's amazing stats in the right-hand bar.

TORQUE
2,015 lb-ft
(2,732 Nm)

FLAMING TAKE-OFF

Top Fuel drag racing is all about intense acceleration. Using nitromethane engines, cars reach incredible speeds in the blink of an eye and cover the 1,000-foot (305m) straight track in just 3.7 seconds! Nitromethane, which has been used to fuel rockets, burns slower than gasoline/petrol, so the exhausts shoot out flames of burning fuel, adding to the drama.

DON'T MOVE!

One of the most famous Top Fuel dragsters is Tony Schumacher's U.S. Army, painted after its **sponsor**. It's one of the fastest-accelerating machines on land, which has set multiple records and won most of the races it's entered. See its awesome stats to the right.

FIERCE COMPETITION

Top Fuel is incredibly competitive, with racers competing to be named the fastest. Schumacher's U.S. Army may have a successful history, but it's now been swept off the top spot by newer and faster cars.

POWER
10-11,000 hp

**0-336 MPH
(0-541 KM/H)**
3.7 seconds

TOP SPEED
337 mph
(542 km/h)

ENGINE
Supercharged
Chrysler Hemi
engine

TORQUE
Unknown

OVERPOWERED STRENGTH

Top Fuel cars are so powerful that dynamometers – the machines used to work out a car's torque – can't handle the strength. That's why torque is either unknown or has to be guessed!

FASTER THAN SOUND

People once thought it was impossible to fly faster than sound. When planes did fly near the speed of sound, they would shake and be hard to control – so the speed of sound became known as the sound barrier. But in October 1947, the Bell X-1, piloted by Chuck Yeager, broke safely through this barrier – flying faster than sound for the first time.

MAKING HISTORY

The Bell X-1 was an experimental plane, powered by a rocket and shaped like a machine-gun bullet. For its historic flight, it was carried into the air beneath a B-29 bomber. Nearly 4 miles up (almost 6.5 km), the bomber dropped the X-1. At once, Yeager fired the rocket and blasted the X-1 away. Within minutes, he had broken through the sound barrier!

On one flight six years after breaking the sound barrier, Yeager's plane went into a rapid, uncontrollable spin as it dived. His head was flung against the cockpit canopy, cracking the canopy. Luckily, he was able to regain control just in time.

IT GOES BOOM!

People on the ground certainly knew Yeager had broken the sound barrier. When a plane flies very fast, it pushes up waves of pressure in the air in front, like the waves in front of a boat. These waves travel at the speed of sound, but Yeager's plane was flying faster. So his plane began to scrunch them up ahead of it into one giant shock wave. Eventually, the shock wave burst like a paper bag, sending out a loud sound called a sonic boom.

POWER
XLR-11
liquid-fuel
rocket

LAUNCH SYSTEM
Drop launch
from B-29

TOP SPEED
957 mph
(1,540 km/h)

MACH SPEED
1.45

MAX ALTITUDE
Over 13 miles
(22 km)

SPACE STREAKER

Imagine going around the world in less than two hours. That's how fast the DARPA Falcon HTV-2 rocket-launched, unmanned glider could fly! Like the Bell X-1, it had to be carried high in the air by a rocket before gliding back to Earth. It was an experimental project designed to discover the secrets to flying at **hypersonic** speeds. While it reached a mind-blowing 13,000 mph (20,921 km/h), it soon lost communication and crashed. Engineers are yet to perfect it.

FLIGHT PLAN

Like a spacecraft, the HTV-2 was carried up to the edge of space inside the nose of a rocket, which was launched from Vandenberg Air Force Base in California. Then, high above the Pacific, the rocket's nose opened to release the glider, which flew back to Earth at hypersonic speeds.

Protective
launch shell

Minotaur IV Lite
rocket launcher

POWER
None
(as it's a
glider)

LAUNCH SYSTEM
Minotaur IV
Lite rocket
(see left)

TOP SPEED
13,000 mph
(20,921 km/h)

MACH SPEED
20

LAUNCH ALTITUDE
100 miles
(161 km)

SMASHING SOUND

A plane that flies faster than the speed of sound is said
to be "**supersonic**". But when it flies more than five
times faster than sound, it is called "hypersonic". HTV
stands for Hypersonic Technology Vehicle – and HTV-
2's flight was 20 times faster than the speed of sound!
It was so fast that temperatures on the glider's body
reached 3,500°F (1,926°C) within minutes – so hot that
its skin disintegrated, which is why it crashed.

BLACK LIGHTNING

NASA's X-43A - also known as Hyper-X - was the fastest powered plane ever! Like the HTV-2, the X-43A was an experimental plane launched from mid-air that flew only once. Three X-43As were built. The first failed in mid-flight. The second shattered the world speed record for a jet plane in 2004, reaching 5,000 mph (8,046 km/h). Later in 2004, the third screeched through the air at 7,000 mph (11,265 km/h)!

ROCKET-LAUNCHED

It's not easy launching an X-43A. It's attached to the booster rocket and carried high up in the air by a B-52 bomber. 8 miles (almost 13 km) up, the B-52 releases the booster rocket. In a matter of seconds, the rocket shoots the X-43A a further 12 miles (19 km) up before falling away to leave the X-43A to make its high-speed flight.

SCRAMJET POWER

The X-43A is powered by a Supersonic **Combustion** Ramjet, or Scramjet for short. Unlike conventional jets, which have fan blades to draw in air and compress it, scramjets have no moving parts. Instead, air is simply scooped up and rammed into the engine as the plane flies forward at supersonic speed. This supersonic air is ignited with fuel to produce the engine's mighty thrust (see diagram below).

POWER
Scramjet

LAUNCH SYSTEM
B-52 plane

TOP SPEED
7,000 mph
(11,265 km/h)

MACH SPEED
9.6

LAUNCH ALTITUDE
20 miles
(32 km)

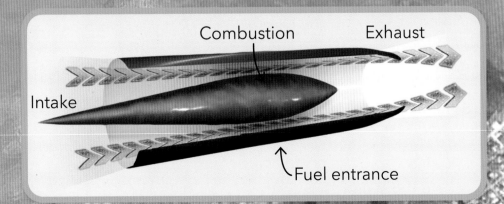

Combustion   Exhaust

Intake

Fuel entrance

ROCKET SPEED

Both the HTV-2 and the X-43A were unmanned aircraft. The highest and fastest-ever piloted flights were achieved in X-15 rocket planes. In 1963, pilot Joseph Walker took an X-15 more than 65 miles (105 km) up to the very edge of space. This was so high that it qualified him as an astronaut!

FLYING HIGH

Like the X-43A, the X-15 was carried high into the sky by a big B-52 bomber, the Stratofortress, and then dropped. At once, the X-15's rocket engine would burst into life and blast the plane even further into the outer atmosphere. The X-15 flew so high and so fast that the wing flaps used to control direction on ordinary planes would have had no effect. So when the pilot moved his joystick, he was actually controlling little rocket thrusters!

POWER
XLR-99
rocket engine

LAUNCH SYSTEM
B-52 plane

TOP SPEED
4,520 mph
(7,274 km/h)

MACH SPEED
6.7

MAX ALTITUDE
67 miles
(108 km)

PILOT'S VIEW

The canopy of the X-15's cockpit was largely metal with just a small window for the pilot to see out of. Only three X-15s were ever made, and only one flew at any time. So, the view of the X-15 outside the window in this image shows what it would look like if two did fly together!

THE BLACKBIRD

Shaped like a dagger to reduce its visibility to radar, the Lockheed SR-71 Blackbird was the ultimate spy plane. If it was ever spotted and shot at, its speed allowed it to outrun any missile. In fact, it was the fastest jet plane ever, able to reach 2,193 mph (3,529 km/h).

SHH...

The Blackbird was built in secret with all kinds of advanced technology and materials. It was the first "stealth" plane, covered with a special paint to disguise it from radar. To cope with searing temperatures generated by friction in the upper atmosphere, it was made almost entirely of titanium. This meant it could cope with temperatures of up to 950°F (510°C).

FINAL FLIGHT

The Blackbird was in operation from 1964 to 1998, and a total of 32 were built. One is now in the Smithsonian Institution in Chantilly, Virginia (USA). In 1990, pilots Lt. Col. Ed Yielding and Lt. Col. Joseph Vida set a speed record by flying from Los Angeles to Washington, D.C., in 64 minutes, averaging an amazing 2,124 mph (3,418 km/h).

POWER
Two Pratt and Whitney J58 engines

LAUNCH SYSTEM
Normal take-off

TOP SPEED
2,193 mph (3,529 km/h)

MACH SPEED
3.2

MAX ALTITUDE
16 miles (26 km)

FOXBAT

All of the high-speed planes featured so far were made in tiny numbers. Not the Russian MiG-25. Nearly 1,200 of them were built! Nicknamed the Foxbat, the MiG-25 was extremely rugged and functional as well as fast. It was designed as a fighter with powerful radar to see through enemy stealth systems, but most MiG-25s were used for reconnaissance.

FOXED

Foxbat was the code name that **NATO** gave the MiG-25. They gave all fighter aircraft names beginning with F, and bombers names beginning with B. There is no such animal as a foxbat, but the word combines the cunning of a fox with the stealth of a bat. The flying fox is the world's largest bat, found in the tropical forests of Madagascar, Australia and across Asia.

FOXBAT V BLACKBIRD

The Mikoyan-Gurevich MiG-25 was created by the Soviet Union in 1964 to combat the Blackbird (page 48) – and is almost as fast. It rarely flew at its maximum speed of Mach 3.2 (2,170 mph/3,492 km/h), since the engines were likely to blow up at that speed! Instead, it comfortably cruised at Mach 2.8 (1,920 mph/3,090 km/h). Luckily, the Foxbat and Blackbird never met in combat.

POWER
Two Tumansky turbojet engines

LAUNCH SYSTEM
Normal take-off

TOP SPEED
2,170 mph (3,492 km/h) if you're brave

MACH SPEED
2.8 or (disastrously) 3.2

MAX ALTITUDE
23 miles (37 km)

WHIRLING PROPELLERS

The fastest planes are shot through the air by jets and rockets. But some planes driven only by whirling propellers can really move, too. In World War II, fighter planes such as the British Spitfire and the German Focke-Wulf Fw 190 ripped through the skies at over 400 mph (644 km/h). Toward the end of the war, the American Grumman company created the F8F Bearcat, one of the most powerful propeller planes ever.

GRIZZLY BEAR

The Bearcat is still popular with air racers for its acrobatic ability and amazing turn of speed. In 1969, air racer Lyle Shelton found a wrecked Bearcat, lovingly rebuilt it and named it Rare Bear. In 1989, Shelton flew Rare Bear at a world record speed for piston-engined aircraft. Check out its stats on the right!

POWER
Wright R-3350
radial engine

LAUNCH SYSTEM
Normal runway
take-off

TOP SPEED
528 mph
(850 km/h)

MACH SPEED
Not fast
enough to
measure!

GALLOPING MUSTANGS!

Bearcats are not the only wartime fighters still ripping it up in air races. One of the biggest races of all time was between air racers in modified P-51 Mustangs. Steven Hinton flew Voodoo and his rival, Bill "Tiger" Destefani, flew Strega. Dating from the 1940s, both planes were more than 70 years old but raced at speeds well over 490 mph (789 km/h).

ALTITUDE CLIMB
0-1.9 miles
(3 km) in 91.9
seconds

SUPERSONIC LUXURY

Nowadays, only military pilots can fly faster than sound. But between 1969 and 2003, ordinary people could beat the sound barrier, too, if they flew on the supersonic jet airliner Concorde. A normal flight from London to New York lasts up to eight hours. On Concorde, the flight was less than three and a half hours! But Concorde was heavy on fuel and expensive to run, and in 2003 it was retired from service.

DROOP SNOOT

To keep **air resistance** to a minimum, Concorde was very slim, with a really long, pointed nose. The nose would have made it hard for the crew to see the runway, so it was designed to hinge down for take-off and landing. This was nicknamed a droop snoot.

POWER
Four Rolls-Royce/
Snecma Olympus
turbojet engines

LAUNCH SYSTEM
Normal runway
take-off

TOP SPEED
1,350 mph
(2,173 km/h)

MACH SPEED
2.04

MAX ALTITUDE
11 miles
(18 km)

RUSSIAN RIVAL

In 1977 and 1978, Concorde briefly had an even faster
rival, the Russian Tu-144, although it only flew in the
Soviet Union. Both the Tu-144 and Concorde had
unmistakable triangular or "delta" wings. Delta wings
are not so efficient at lifting planes at low speeds, but
at supersonic speed they give much better stability and
control than conventional wings.

SKY RACERS

For sheer speed and thrills, nothing can beat air racing, the world's fastest motorsport. Right in front of spectators, some of the world's most daring pilots whip their planes in and out of 80-foot-high (24 m) inflatable pylons known as air gates. The aircraft swoop, bank, turn, roll and perform tricky movements with astonishing agility as pilots race to achieve the fastest times.

RED BULL REVELS

One of the best-known series of races is Red Bull Air Race World Championship, which wowed air racing fans for over 15 years. A course of pylons was laid out over water, and 10-15 pilots competed by flying one by one through the pylons against the clock. They raced small aerobatic planes, such as the Zivko Edge 540, with top speeds of 265 mph (426 km/h). See more stats in the right-hand bar!

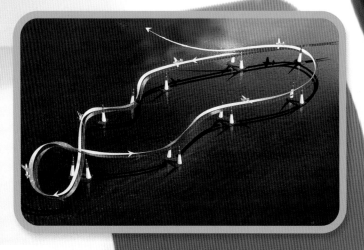

RENO ROARERS

At the yearly air races held at Reno in Nevada, USA, for over 60 years, there was an "Unlimited Class" race, which any piston engine, propeller-driven plane could enter. The race was dominated by modified World War II fighters that roared around the oval course at speeds of about 500 mph (805 km/h). In the "Sport Class" for home-built planes in 2009, Curt Brown hit 543.6 mph (875 km/h) in his jet-engined Viper. What a record!

POWER
Lycoming
piston engine

LAUNCH SYSTEM
Normal runway
take-off

TOP SPEED
265 mph
(426 km/h)

CLIMB RATE
3,700 ft
(1,128 m)
per minute

ROLL RATE
420 degrees
per second

TRUCK RACERS

When truck racing took off in the 1980s, the racers were just the cabs of big road-going trucks. Unhooked from their trailers, the cabs could race along at speeds of up to 150 mph (241 km/h). People found the sight of these monsters tearing around a track so exciting that the sport caught on. Nowadays, the trucks are purpose-built racers that will never haul load.

RACING RULES

Racing trucks are built to very specific technical requirements to ensure fair competition. They also have to be limited to 100 mph (161 km/h) to keep the sport safe. With such massive trucks hurtling along so close together, crashes do happen, but thankfully they are very rare!

POWER
Up to
1,500 hp

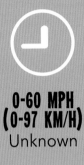

**0-60 MPH
(0-97 KM/H)**
Unknown

TOP SPEED
Limited to
100 mph
(161 km/h)

ENGINE
Six cylinder
turbo-charged

TORQUE
Over 4,055 lb-ft (5,500 Nm)

CHASING CHAMPIONSHIPS

The biggest, most competitive racing series is the Goodyear **FIA** Truck Racing Championship, which has been running since 1985. Every year, over 400,000 spectators gather to watch the world's most professional racing teams and drivers go head to head for the championship title!

MASSIVE MONSTERS

Who said wheels have to be small? Monster trucks have giant wheels, massive suspension and super-powerful engines. That means they can charge over obstacles, like cars, and perform breathtaking stunts. No wonder millions of people turn up to Monster Jam events. Inspired by the first monster truck, Bigfoot, these trucks keep pushing the limits to get bigger and more powerful.

FLYING TRUCK!

Monster trucks compete ferociously for the longest jump. But Joe Sylvester's "Bad Habit" soars the farthest of all. In 2013, Bad Habit charged up the launch ramp then hurtled over 237 ft (72 m) through the air before almost landing on its nose. That leap demolished the previous world record and will take some beating!

RAMINATOR

When brothers Tim and Mark Hall set out to build the Raminator, they didn't just want a stunt master – they wanted a truck with superpowers. What they came up with was the world's fastest monster truck. Raminator reached a sensational world record 99 mph (159 km/h) in 2014, ripping up the Circuit of the Americas in Texas (USA), but has since been beaten by Bad Habit. See more stats for superpowered Raminator in the right-hand bar.

POWER
Over 2,000 hp

**0-60 MPH
(0-97 KM/H)**
Under
3 seconds

TOP SPEED
99 mph
(159 km/h)

ENGINE
565cl
supercharged
Hemi engine

TORQUE
Unknown

WHERE'S THE FIRE?

You want firefighters to get to fires fast - but none can match the speed of Shannen Seydel's incredible fire truck called Hawaiian Eagle. In 1995, firefighter Seydel took the water tank out of a 1940s Ford fire truck - and slotted in two turbojet engines in its place to create the world's fastest fire truck. With flames shooting out behind, it certainly looks like the coolest fire truck, but it's not used for firefighting!

JET PROPULSION

All jet engines work by drawing air in with a huge fan. As the fan sucks in the air, it squeezes it and mixes it with fuel. The mix is set alight and swells rapidly, shooting out of the back of the engine. The hot air that shoots out hits the air outside and creates thrust - a mighty push that drives the plane (or fire truck!) forward.

FASTEST TRUCK EVER?

In 1998, on a track in Canada, Seydel unleashed his fire-breathing beast. The speed that the Hawaiian Eagle reached was incredible. It reached a scorching 407 mph (655 km/h). That's even faster than Shockwave (see page 66)!

POWER
12,000 hp

**0-60 MPH
(0-97 KM/H)**
Unknown

TOP SPEED
407 mph
(655 km/h)

ENGINE
Two Rolls-Royce Bristol Viper engines

THRUST
12,000 lb

PICKUP RUNNER

You may think a pickup is just for cruising around with a load of supplies. **Hot rodder** Gale Banks will make you think again. His Dodge Dakota Sidewinder pickup doesn't just look as sleek and shiny as a supercar, it's superfast, too! In 2002, it set a world record for a pickup of 217 mph (349 km/h) in a two-way run, and hit a 222 mph (357 km/h) exit speed.

DON'T STEP ON THIS SNAKE!

Sidewinders are venomous snakes that live in the deserts of southwest USA and Mexico. These deadly predators have their own special way of moving over the loose desert sand. Instead of moving forward, they whip sideways so fast that they can be hard to see. It's a fitting name for the Banks pickup, which whips across the Bonneville Salt Flats in Utah, USA, at high speeds.

POWER
735 hp

0-60 MPH (0-97 KM/H)
3.9 seconds

TOP SPEED
222 mph
(357 km/h)

ENGINE
5.9L
turbo diesel

TORQUE
1,300 lb-ft
(1,762 Nm)

DIESEL DESTROYER

Surprisingly, the Banks Sidewinder uses a diesel engine. Banks Engineering was determined to show that diesels could be just as fast as gas/petrol engines. It squeezed 735 hp out of a Cummins diesel engine with a special "variable geometry" turbocharger.

FASTER THAN A JET PLANE

One of the most powerful trucks ever has to be Les Shockley's Shockwave. From the front it looked like an ordinary 1984 Peterbilt truck. But mounted on the back were three massive jet engines that blasted the fire-breathing monster from a standstill to 300 mph (483 km/h) in just 11 seconds. It could actually reach a scorching 376 mph (605 km/h)!

FLAMING FURY

Father and son Neal and Chris Darnell rebuilt Shockwave in 2012, adding features that would make it steal any show it entered! The flames that gushed from the twin exhaust stacks on the cab weren't really part of the jet. They were fed with raw diesel fuel, then electrically ignited to produce spectacular flame effects.

CATCH THAT JET!

In demonstrations at air shows, a jet fighter would fly low over a standing Shockwave. Instantly the monster truck roared to life. Within just a quarter of a mile, it had not only caught up with the plane but actually overtaken it! The truck had brakes, but it also threw out parachutes to help it slow down. Sadly, in 2022, Shockwave crashed during a show due to a mechanical failure, causing driver Chris to lose his life.

POWER
36,000 hp

**0-300 MPH
(0-483 KM/H)**
11 seconds

TOP SPEED
376 mph
(605 km/h)

ENGINE
Three J34-48
jet engines

THRUST
21,000 lb
(more than
9,500 kg)

FAST AND WILD

Off-roaders are meant to be rugged and ready for any kind of terrain. They're not meant to be fast. Well, think again. Ford's F-150 SVT Raptor is a pickup that's both tough in the mud and megafast on roads. Powered by a big V8 engine and impressive suspension, it's built to cope with anything, from desert sand to rocky boulders to fresh snow!

BIRD OF PREY

Ford's Raptor gets its name from a family of birds called raptors – birds of prey that include hawks, eagles, falcons and vultures. These fantastic flyers have super sharp eyes for spotting prey from high up. Swooping down from above, they grasp their prey with their curved talons and rip off flesh with their hooked beaks.

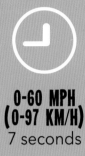

POWER
411 hp

**0-60 MPH
(0-97 KM/H)**
7 seconds

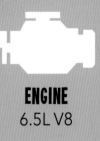

TOP SPEED
Limited to
100 mph
(161 km/h)

ENGINE
6.5L V8

TORQUE
434 lb-ft
(588 Nm)

TOUGH IN THE DIRT

There are plenty of fast vehicles on the world's roads, but very few speed machines could handle such extreme off-road conditions as the Raptor. Key to its off-road abilities are a rugged build, four-wheel drive and long travel suspension. The driver even has "Hill Descent Control". This adjusts braking and acceleration automatically to keep the Raptor's speed steady when coming down steep banks.

ROAD RACER

For an amazing moment in time, the world's fastest accelerating street-legal car wasn't a Lamborghini or Bugatti supercar, but a pickup truck. In 2014, Larry Larson's 1998 Chevy S-10 covered a quarter-mile from a standing start in 6 seconds, reaching 244 mph (393 km/h). You won't see this superfast truck much on the road, though. It's a drag racer, built for displaying its might on the strip.

TRUCK TREATMENT

Larson's S-10 gets its power from a Brodix Chevy engine so mighty that the hood/bonnet needs a bulge to fit it in. The S-10 has two fuel systems: gas/petrol for the road and pure alcohol for the drag track. To save weight on the drag track, the gas/petrol system is removed and the truck's heavy steel doors are replaced with lighter doors.

SLICK TACTICS

Before each drag race, drivers perform burnouts by spinning their wheels really fast. This gives good grip or "traction" between the wheels and the track, meaning the engine's power is used to maximum effect to push the dragster forward.

POWER
3,300 hp

**0-244 MPH
(0-393 KM/H)**
6 seconds

TOP SPEED
244 mph
(393 km/h)

ENGINE
10,000 cc
twin turbo

TORQUE
Unknown

SCHOOL'S OUT

School Time may look pretty much like any other school bus, but it's a one-of-a-kind speed machine! With the help of his Indy Boys team, car fanatic and designer Paul Stender stripped out all the seats and replaced them with a 42,000 hp fighter-jet engine that can blast the old bus up to 367 mph (591 km/h) in a matter of seconds!

GHOST SPEED

School Time is not a real bus, of course. A real bus couldn't stand the stresses of moving at such high speeds. School Time was hand-built to look like a bus, using special metals that could cope with extreme speeds and temperatures. School Time shoots out 80-foot (24-m) flames as it screams down the runway, burning an incredible amount of fuel in a single run.

GHOST SPEED

School Time uses the same engine as the McDonnell Phantom F-4, which was one of the fastest and most successful jet fighters of the last century, operating from 1960 to 1996. It was famous for the powerful jet engines that helped it climb at breathtaking speeds. In 1961, a Phantom hurtled through the sky at 1,606.3 mph (2,585 km/h) – just one of the amazing world records it set!

POWER
42,000 hp

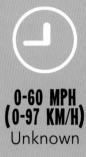

**0-60 MPH
(0-97 KM/H)**
Unknown

TOP SPEED
367 mph
(591 km/h)

ENGINE
General Electric
J79 jet engine

THRUST
Around
17,000 lb-ft
(23,049 Nm)

UNBELIEVABLE FAST FACTS

WILD RECORDS

In 1964, Craig Breedlove thought he had set a new car land speed record of 526 mph (846 km/h) in his three-wheeled, jet-propelled Spirit of America. But at the time, the FIA rules for land speed records required four wheels! His win was actually classed as a new motorcycle record, awarded by the **FIM** instead of the FIA.

HIGH-SPEED DRAGSTER

The U.S. Army Top Fuel Dragster accelerates faster than any other car on the planet, covering 1,000 feet (305 m) in less than 4 seconds. That means the G-forces when it takes off from the start are huge. The driver feels a force of 5G – that's five times the force of gravity. When they throw out the parachutes to slow down, they experience a force of 5G the other way!

SMART STARTER

The smoothness and power of the Honda Blackbird's engine depends on its 3D computer-mapped ignition system. This ensures that ignition (the spark that sets the fuel alight) occurs at the best possible moment. It factors in how hard the engine is working, whereas normal systems usually just base their timings according to engine speed only.

WORLD'S FASTEST

The official speed record for a vehicle powered through its wheels is 458 mph (737 km/h) by the turbine-powered Vesco Turbinator, driven by Don Vesco in 2001. Thrust SSC, the car that set the absolute land speed record, was jet-powered, meaning the jet's thrust powered it forward, not the wheels. Although the newest Turbinator model has exceeded 500 mph (805 km/h), it hasn't been verified for a new world record...yet!

SUPER NINJA

The Kawasaki H2R Ninja's fairing is not just a glamorous piece of styling. It was developed with lots of testing in a wind tunnel, which ensured the bike was streamlined to reduce drag. The designers also gave it little winglets that use the airflow to force the front wheel down onto the road and improve grip.

TOP SPOT

The most famous place in the world for land speed record attempts is Bonneville Salt Flats in the USA. It's a natural flat formed by salty water evaporating to leave a vast, smooth crust of salt. It's where George Easton and John Cobb competed in the 1930s and where Craig Breedlove claimed his titles in the 1960s.

HIGH-SPEED LUXURY

Most of the world's fastest planes are used for military purposes. But if you're mega rich, you can still fly very fast in a Cessna Citation X: the world's fastest passenger plane. It can only carry 12 people, but it slices through the air at over 700 mph (Mach 0.9), close to the speed of sound.

THEN AND NOW

The first big truck race was held in June 1979 at the Atlanta Motor Speedway in the USA, and the idea quickly caught on, thanks to its feature in the 1977 movie *Smokey and the Bandit*. There are now truck races all over the world, and most major truck manufacturers have their own racing team.

EXTREME EXPERIMENTS

The Bell X-1, which broke the sound barrier for the first time, was the first of the USA's X planes. X stands for experimental, and they are all unique planes designed to try out new ideas. Many were developed in top-secret conditions! There have been more than 50 different X-plane projects just in the USA.

BIG IDEAS

One of the best places to see pickups racing bumper to bumper is in the NASCAR Truck series. NASCAR stands for National Association for Stock Car Auto Racing, and the idea of the series dates to the early 1990s, when a group of off-road pickup truck racers decided to compete on a proper paved track, as in Formula One racing.

RECORD-BREAKING DISAGREEMENTS

The experimental X-15A-2 became the fastest rocket-powered aircraft after reaching 4,520 mph (7,274 km/h), or Mach 6.7, when flown over California (USA) in October 1967 by USAF pilot Major William "Pete" Knight. Despite achieving almost double the official FAI air speed record of 2,193 mph (3,529 km/h), the X-15A-2 isn't eligible for the record of fastest manned aircraft because it did not take off and land using its own power. That record belongs to the Lockheed SR-71.

AMAZING STUNTS

As well as being megafast, some truck drivers are brave thrill seekers and perform amazing stunts. The current world record for the longest pickup truck jump is over 379 feet (115 m). That's like jumping over a row of 10 school buses in one jump! Stunt drivers are always trying to beat world records – who knows what will be achieved next...

DRIVERS HALL OF FAME

Whether competing in races, performing stunts, or testing the power of new models, the people who drive these megafast vehicles are amazingly brave and talented. Let's look at some iconic people and their legendary achievements.

RACING BIKE DRIVER HALL OF FAME

VALENTINO ROSSI

Italian racing rider Valentino Rossi may be one of the most admired motorcycle riders of all time. He started riding from a very young age, and won his first Grand Prix race at the age of just 17. When the top-class MotoGP was introduced in 2002, Rossi won eleven of the sixteen races. He has since been World Champion nine times.

CAR DRIVERS HALL OF FAME

JUAN FANGIO

Some say the greatest racing driver of all time was Argentinian Juan Fangio, who raced in the 1950s when Grand Prix racing was brutally dangerous.

MICHAEL SCHUMACHER

Others think the best racing driver is German Michael Schumacher, who scored 91 wins between 1991 and 2012.

AYRTON SENNA

It's also said that Brazilian Ayrton Senna is the best racing driver. He won 41 titles before being tragically killed during a high-speed Grand Prix crash in 1994, aged 34.

IN THE SKY HALL OF FAME

APOLLO 11

The record for fastest speed achieved by humans goes to the crew of Apollo 10, who went on a mission to the Moon. Thomas P. Stafford, Eugene Cernan and John Young reached an incredible speed of 24,790 mph (39,895 km/h) in the command module of Apollo 10 on their return flight to Earth in May 1969!

TRUCK DRIVERS HALL OF FAME

JOCHEN HAHN

Jochen's dad, Konrad, was also a champion truck racer, but in 1999 Konrad had a bad crash, and Jochen became the Hahn racing team's lead driver. His results got better and better, and in 2011, 2012, and 2013, the team was the FIA European Truck Racing champion three times in a row!

NORBERT KISS

Another top name is Norbert Kiss, a Hungarian motorsports professional who has driven for different teams over the years. A super speedster, Kiss is a five-time European Truck Racing champion.

GLOSSARY

Accelerate - (verb) to speed up. In this book, this mostly refers to vehicles accelerating from a complete standstill.

Air resistance - a kind of friction that occurs between air and another object. When an object faces a lot of air resistance, it will find it harder to move through the air.

Altitude - the distance of an object above a surface. Planes' altitude is usually measured in comparison with sea level.

cc - this number refers to the size of a vehicle's engine. The bigger the cc number, the more powerful the engine.

Combustion - the scientific term for "burning": a chemical reaction of fuel with oxygen which produces heat and light.

FIA - Fédération Internationale de l'Automobile - the company that watches over motorsports around the world and sets rules so that events are safe and fair.

FIM - Fédération Internationale de Motocyclisme - the company that watches over motorcycle racing around the world and sets rules so that events are safe and fair.

Formula 1 (F1) - a huge international racing series for single-seater racing cars which is held annually.

Fujita scale - a rating system which shows how strong a tornado is, based on wind speed and damage.

Horsepower (hp) - this number shows the maximum power direct from the vehicle's engine; 1 horsepower can move 550 pounds one foot every second, written as 550 ft-lb per second.

Hot rodder - someone who drives a motor vehicle that has been specially modified to give it extra power or speed.

Hypersonic - something that moves faster than five times the speed of sound.

Mach speed - a measurement of the speed of an object compared to the speed of sound. Mach 1 is equal to the speed of sound.

Monocoque - a type of motorcycle framing where the outer shell helps to hold all the internal pieces together and shares the weight and stresses of the frame.

Naturally aspirated - a type of engine which takes in air normally, without the use of a turbo or supercharger.

NATO - the North Atlantic Treaty Organization - a group of countries that have promised to defend each other if any of them is attacked.

Nm - Newton meter/metre is a measurement of torque (see right)

Protective fairing - parts of a motorcycle which protect the driver's hands, legs, and feet, keep them out of the wind and reduce air resistance (see left).

Reconnaissance - a mission used to find out information.

Rolling sculpture - a vehicle that is designed to be an artistic masterpiece, rather than a practical vehicle to be driven.

Sponsor - a company that pays someone to advertise their company. In sports, a sportsperson or athlete may wear clothing or drive a vehicle with the sponsor company's logo on it.

Supercharger - a device that boosts an engine's power by using the engine to turn a fan that forces extra air and fuel into the cylinders.

Supersonic - something that moves faster than the speed of sound.

Torque - the force with which something turns, measured in pounds per feet (lb-ft) or Newton meters/metres (Nm).

Turbocharger - a device that boosts an engine's power by using the exhaust gases to turn a turbine that rams extra fuel and air into the cylinders.

INDEX